INSTAGRAM MARKETING

Complete guide of 2018. Discover the 27

secrets of marketing on Instagram

Philip J Luise

Disclaimer

All the material contained in this book is provided for educational and informational purposes only. No responsibility can be taken for any results or outcomes resulting from the use of this material. While every attempt has been made to provide information that is both accurate and effective, the author does not assume any responsibility for the accuracy or use/misuse of this information.

Table of Contents

Introduction

Businesses using Instagram to promote their products, services and offers now have an even greater opportunity to market their wares to a super targeted audience. With the backing of Facebook. Instagram has launched its advertising platform that integrates with Facebook's amazing targeting capabilities and businesses are taking full advantage. Businesses know that users are watching their news feed. As a result. Instagrammers are 2.5 times more likely to click on newsfeed ads than ads on any other social media platform. So running Instagram ads for your business opens up a world of opportunity.

More importantly Instagram's ad platform is easy to use, it's fun and bubbling over with passionate and enthusiastic users. It has excellent metrics and is still affordable for small businesses. If you are already advertising your product with social media ads or trying to build your list then integrating Instagram ads into your marketing mix is essential.

However, it should be noted that Instagram can work better for some businesses than others. It has more than 800 million monthly users, and is continuing to grow. And, because it's part of Facebook, you know there is huge pressure for it to succeed.

Instagram is a highly visual social marketing platform. If you're a service provider, you can post a range of pictures to help convey your brand and value proposition. However, when you can really show off is if you have physical products and a sound Instagram marketing strategy which will definitely help to boost sales and profits.

Just like any other social network, good results come from increasing your following on a constant basis. The more people who network with your posts and brand, the larger your potential audience for each post.

Instagram and Instagram ads provide you with that opportunity to connect with the people in your niche in a fun, visual way. It easy to use if you have a smartphone. Take a photo, upload it, and your followers will see it and be able to interact with it.

We all understand that a smooth social network needs value-added service and just as Rome was not built in a day: Instagram too improvised and made new and important changes in a specific period. It made the network so famous that the year 2017 witnessed a whopping 600 million of users (monthly) and daily users exceeding over 400 million. In the past few months, another 2 million insta lovers was added making a remarkable progress in its publicity.

It was successful in dethroning the ever popular Facebook who ruled the search engines since 2004. Its level of engagement is 52 times more than Facebook, and 127 times higher than twitter. Instagram made striking changes and they are still making these changes to attract the huge attention of aspiring and ruling business populace who make millions by advertising their products on this websites.

In this book, I am going to discuss with you the 27 secrets of marketing on Instagram. Like every social media platform, you'll be wasting your time if you fail to recognize the hidden secrets of social media marketing peculiar to that platform. The way you advertise on Twitter is quite different from Facebook and Instagram. That is why you need to learn the hidden *algorithms* (if such exists) and tactics in creating a successful ad.

Understand The Concept

Of Instagram Ad

Okay, so now we are down to Business. Instagram is a great step to advertise and explode your business to millions of users. However, we should understand that there exists different ad for different purposes. There are carousel ads, photo ads and video ads that can open up your business areas and capture a precise audience to promote the product.

Carousel Ads: Just like the photo ads, the carousel features shows multiple pictures a user can leaf through. This is a good place for you to show your potential clients/buyers how unique you are with your product or service. I have made my research and most times I see people who have online stores posting a lot of pictures of the same shoe or clothes using the carousel ad. This is just a total waste of efforts. People want to feel your stock through the screen of their phones. You don't just post the same picture snapped differently, you make it interesting buy having several pictures of different products. If you have the same kind of product but different colors remember to use the space meant for typing to mention that it "comes in different colors and sizes".

Video Ads: With patronized label on top, this feature should be used to post beautiful video post that can instantly grab a user's attention. And the funny thing about video ads is that it doesn't matter who you're marketing to, whoever they are, wherever they live, whatever job they have-research has been able to show us that they love video content. It is very engaging and easy to process mentally. Online, video hogs more than an hour of our day, and 50% of all internet traffic. In fact, by 2019, that number is projected to grow to 80%. If you are still indecisive, check the statistics.

Photo Ads: With the advice of learning more button on top of the post, this feature is a regular photo post that can visually appeal to the audience and make them see your product in detail.

Mistakes People Make During

Instagram Marketing

The main mistake made by marketers is in posting things online without a *call to action.* Okay, I have been able to see the product. Wow, it looks cute, what else? Instagrammers are quick to scroll through while they hit the like button for something they really enjoy. Your goal should be that, you want them to see the ad? Like it, comment with questions on how they could get your product or services. How can you do this? You should set an objective for each post and use the objective to establish your call to action, for example "register now" or "buy now."

In addition, Instagram marketers are also fond of over-posting. Please, don't fall into this trap. Choose two time spots, day and evening, and see when most of your engagement occurs. Then add posts steadily, or reduce your posting if you are getting a smaller amount of engagement.

Another common mistake is that they fail to use the Analytics. The analytics on Instagram allows your business to see how well your various campaigns are working. You have to convert to a business account to access the tools. The tools will then help you have

an understanding of how your followers are engaging

with your content, so you can get better results.

Secrets To Instagram Marketing

#1 Get The Basics Right: What are the basics? The Kind of Instagram account you need, your followers, your following and your post. For marketing sake, you should make sure to fill out your business profile and bio on your business Instagram account. Make sure to use a clear crisp version of your company logo as your profile picture. The importance of pictures cannot be overrated when it comes to Instagram. Have a good graphic designer to do this for you. Instagram can't be Instagram without good pictures. In fact, having good quality pictures is also one of the basics. You choose a username and profile picture that represents your firm but you can upgrade that any time. For your bio, you should think about your target audience. Write something that would tell them (potential clients or customers) what they should expect in your post

Furthermore, your username, profile-(public or private account), posts, hashtag, photo map, tagging, direct posts, explore tab, News feed, activity feed etc. are very important. We would cover all of this as we move on.

#2 Mirror Your Brand Through Handles: Your Instagram handle is the same as your username. There is this popular trend of having the same name throughout all social media platforms. This is very good because it makes it easy for users to get to know you better. For example, you can have the username-*livingspring_au* on Instagram, twitter and Facebook.

Putting an instant handle and customized hashtags on your services and products would urge your customers to tag you whenever they share something from your enterprise. It can be a product, a service, or a tourist place where you take people to their destinations. It is beneficial for you and other users who would want to know about you and find you easily. Being a leader of your brand, you must also be responsible to comment like and mention the names of the customers who mirror your bran by giving positive feedbacks.

#3 A Hashtag Business: Like Twitter and Even Facebook. Instagram is heavy on hashtags. By means of hashtags your business or brand promotion would create miracles for your profit margin. Cool impressive and relevant hashtags will not only popularize your profile but also expand the promotions across the virtual geographical boundaries. Take for example this logo of your services #fitnessAndTraining this works as a hashtag. But #Fitness&Training does not. Users can search for hashtag and if they find it relevant, they click on it and browse for few moments. Therefore, it is mandatory that you use effective hashtags to be an eye candy for users. Hashtags are used mainly to find and give context to your post or comment. One of the many uses of hashtag on Instagram like we have mentioned is targeted social media marketing. This is when businesses will target Instagram followers to either gain followers, increase comments, likes, or even leads. You should use the Instagram search function to see what other Instagram companies and brands and posting and what users are responding too. With this, you can now create a customized hashtag marketing campaign dedicated to people in this specific niche.

Remember, using more than 30 hashtags for your brand can create confusion for the customers. They should be unique, creative and few in number. It will help you to grab genuine people who would not just interact but would buy or promote your product.

#4 Pictures and Selfies videos: Real and non-filtered pictures and selfies grab the highest attention from the virtual crowd. Also, you should learn to upgrade your look. Images are everything on Instagram so make your images and video look GREAT. Savvy Instagram users want to see "beautiful" or read "funny" or relate to something meaningful. Use apps and other image/video tools to upgrade the look and feel of everything you post on Instagram.

A selfie video about your product would turn heads. It is behind the scene process, where you ask your audience about your services, your food items, or the post pictures of your most popular product. Create a demo video of the machinery, it it is connected with automobile field or show the exquisite restaurant, kitchen, saloon or whatever you are running. Create a shout-out video, post it, and see how amazing your feedbacks are.

#5 Personalize Your Brand With Employees: The employees are the backbone of every business institution. You should personalize your brand with your people. Knowing the most personal values and secrets would build an aura of trust in their minds. Include a video or collage of your employees who work earnestly to make you shine through the platform. Let them know your organization is not just a place to work but also a fun-filled place to discover your hidden abilities.

The Instagram account of your employees is as important as the business account. Yes. Make sure you tag them. Everyone must follow the business account and they can also tag the brand's name whenever they post a picture of a video which is intended to promote the brand or the company. A single employee might just have enough followers to turn your business around. Through the tags and comment section you can get more potential clients and customers.

Conclusively, the Instagram account of the company must be this *high and mighty* account which fails to like, comment or follow other users. Just one comment on the post of your employee can go a long way.

#6 Tell Users Why you are on Instagram: Since this is your business account, keep it business, not personal. Help users identify with your brand and just make sure that you are not too *salesey*. Most times, people want to have a break from the; *contact me now for your order, get this now, get that.* They just want to enjoy Instagram like a normally. You should take this into consideration by creating a fun filled post with good pictures, you can also feature a trending topic. All posts shouldn't be about advertising. By telling users why you are on Instagram you are letting them know what to expect, creating such familiarity between you and users and stretching the welcoming arms.

#7 Exclusive Deals & Coupons: No matter how hard we pretend, everyone loves freebies, giveaway, deals and coupons. Yes, you may say it is too cheap and *low class* but we are still excited when we get such offer. The most important thing here is that you should offer something your audience actually wants. If you are offering a discount that isn't enough value for your audience, then it is not going to do very well. You should think towards this line: *first, what would my audience want?* Then ask yourself: *What do I feel comfortable offering?* Then you should find the balance between them.

Excite your customers by posting exclusive discount offers and coupon codes as an incentive of following you. You can share an image or create a coupon code under the item that they are to buy. Other way is you can generate an alternative of asking them to follow you if they wish to buy. It would make them feel embellished and important. Next time you would see their friends of friends and relatives buying the same thing and making positive marks on your business.

#8 Utilize the Instagram stories: Instagram stories allow businesses to interact with their customers and prospects by making a series of images in order to tell a story. Each story you create should enhance your brand and make your value proposition clear.

Another thing to remember about Instagram stories is they're not everlasting. The images and videos remain on your feed for only 24 hours, then disappear, make it worthwhile. Instagram stories can be used for increased brand awareness, getting more subscribers and generating sales. Post your stores at a time you know is popular with your users, in order to make the most of the 24-hour cycle. Sometimes, the Instagram stories don't have to be as polished as the in-feed content. In reality, the ad-hock, *let's stop getting polite and start getting real* nature of the Instagram stories feature is what makes it possible for savvy users to have a break from the glossy visuals and impossibly perfect lifestyle shots.

9 Cross-Promote: Not everybody uses Instagram. Some could possibly have an account but it is inactive. While others are Instagram freaks. A complete campaign is one that should employ all the peculiarities of other social media platforms and not

just focus on one. You should capitalize on each post with a cross-post on Facebook, Twitter, Tumblr, Pinterest, etc. Instagram has made this very simple for you. You should have the Facebook, Twitter and Pinterest button on while you are making a post on Instagram. And through this medium, you can get people to follow you on Instagram from other social media platforms. Cross-promote whenever you can! The trend we have on Instagram now is to *share the love,* by tagging others or even promoting other products and services complementary to yours. Picture it like this: you own a local restaurants which serve beer from the many craft brewers in your area. You as the restaurant owner and the brewers can take full advantage of Instagram by tagging each other. It is a win win for both of you.

#10 Be strategic With Your Bio Link: Instagram is fun and spontaneous when it comes to personal use but if you are using it as a marketing tool, you have to be a little more calculating with it. You should add the link to your website on your bio but make sure you use a link shortener like bit.ly because it would help you monitor the accurate click rates and it is recommended for business purposes. The link in your bio must connect to a landing page which holds the same post you place on Instagram and allows you to collect leads also.

#11. Drive Instagram users into your marketing funnel: For most brands, getting a follow on Instagram is just one step in the overall marketing funnel. You don't just need followers, you need customers, clients, people who are ready to buy your products. Because of this, there is need for you to move your users further down the funnel, you should consider detecting ways to capture your followers' email. Well, the best way to get your followers' email is to ask for it. Sounds cheesy? Yes. Simple and straightforward. This doesn't mean that you slide into the DM of your followers and start asking them for it, you do this strategically.

You share an image with a a call to action in both the caption and visual telling your Instagram followers or users in general to click the link in your bio to download an e-book or sign up for a newsletter. That's it! Once the user takes this action, you'll have the power and freedom to talk with him or her on a one-to-one basis. This would take your connection to the next level. You have to create a beautiful, savvy landing page tailored directly to your Instagram following. Users should feel as if they are still on their Instagram page when they arrive at your landing page.

#12 Leverage Sponsored Ads: This is one of the hottest marketing tips for Instagram right now! The ever growing paid feature on the platform is massive. Today, sponsored ads on Instagram are becoming a regular occurrence on people's timelines and the most exciting thing about it is that whether it is a video or a photo, you would have high number of likes, views and comments. Whether it is one ad or multiple ads using the carousel element, sponsored ad guarantees organic reach.

The sponsored ad feature is giving brands a whole new dimension to target their audience. Previously, only people following the account would see photo updates. But now, brands can promote these to anyone (I mean anyone) within their target audience. However, as a marketer, you should be ready with content that is both engaging and created with a particular target demographic in mind.

#13 Develop an Editorial Calendar: You can access Instagram from your laptop to engage with content from your followers and to update your account with new content. However, we are so much confined to a mobile device such as your tablet or smartphone. For some who work primarily from a laptop, it may be hard for you to make the switch to a tablet or a smartphone especially if you are trying to manage multiple Instagram accounts all at once. To make this transition from laptop to phone smooth, I would recommend that you create an editorial calendar. Creating an editorial calendar means that you plan out your Instagram posts then all you need to do is to create your content and post it to your Instagram. Just like a blog. Besides that, what is great about this is that as your business grows and as you use Instagram more, you'll be able to meet the demands of your business.

#14 Partner with Instagram Influencers: You can't do it alone. Find influencers within your specific vertical who will showcase your products in a fun and innovative way. According to research there are over

40,000 influencers on Instagram covering all verticals, including fashion, beauty, health, wellness, home décor, food and more. Who are the Instagram influencers? They are modern day celebrities who are recognized for their high-quality digital content, large follower base and trusted opinions on the latest products and trends. You should make sure that you align your brand with the right influencers who can expand your brand awareness and follower reach. There are many ways to walk with influencers? You could ask them to help promote your products through giveaways and contests. The Instagram post of the influencer should include the handle of your brand. He/she can either tag it in the photo or in the social media copy. Calls to action must also be included like; SHOP NOW, LEARN MORE ON OUR WEBSITE.

#15 Make graphics Shareworthy: What do we mean by shareworthy? Your graphics should be able to appeal to several people without them getting the notion that you are making an advert. Pairing images with captions is an effective way to engage your audience. Depending on your service and content. It is advisable for you to combine striking graphics with a piece of sharable content, like a stimulating quote or a practical design tip. Make sure you complete the image with a detailed caption and relevant hashtags. You'll have a compelling post overflowing with nuggets of knowledge and information.

#16 Keep It Social: When you use Instagram for business marketing, think social, not ads. Create content your target audience will interact with, not ignore because it looks too spammy. Show that you like pictures in your niche to get people interested in following you.

#17 Provide Value: Instagram users are active shoppers who are doing their research, so the more information you can offer them in terms of images, carousels and stores, the better. Another way you can provide value is by curating the content on your pages and being engaging with followers. Customers want and expect that the content on your page should be relevant to them and your brand. It should be entertaining, engaging and sharable like I have mentioned earlier.

#18 Connect with your followers: Maintaining contact with your customers is vital, particularly for developing business with a small market share. You can start by showing your clients that you are concerned about their feedback. You can achieve this by replying to their questions and comments. This will improve user-generated content and credibility as well as promote the visibility of your products and business. Your Instagram followers can significantly influence the success of your enterprise, and you should never underestimate them.

#19 Be active and consistent: Post at least once daily to keep things up to date and ensure your followers updated with the current happenings. You can experiment posting at varying times of the day to see which time your posts do best. Consistency is crucial in Instagram marketing. Be consistent in your postings and develop a theme that is prominent in your posts. Let your followers know what to expect from you. Your consumers and followers access your accounts to engage with you in a positive (sometimes negative) way or research for your products too. If they see that you have not posted in weeks it would turn them off, decrease your relevancy and also reduce your followers. You should post all the time. If you are tired of posting or you don't have content anymore, you can repost relevant issues and trending topics on Instagram. This would make people to visit your page frequently knowing that it is fun and it is not all about your products.

#20 Create your separate identity: Yes, you want to promote your brand on Instagram but you should have your separate identity. You wouldn't want to look like somebody else or sound like someone else. So first of all, you would have to create your separate identity for your Instagram page. It should be totally different from your personal account. There is no crime in checking the account of others but you should have your own voice, something which makes you unique and different from others.

21 Make Your Account Interesting: When you begin to post. Make sure you choose things that are flattering, interesting and relevant. You can edit your

photos and videos on the app before you post them using Instagram's filters and easy-to-use tools. Use them to make your photos and videos pop. Make sure to add a caption and a few hashtags related to your account and posts so others will see your photos and videos.

#22 Have the right Audience: Does your target market, or even broader potential markets, fall into the demographics that use Instagram? This is another one of those questions that avoids you the pain of talking to a wall online.

It is essential that your customers, past, present, and future, are people who are using the service. If they are not, you will do yourself a great favor by allocating your time and resources to where they are present elsewhere online.

Instagram's users are all those who have been raised in the age of technology. Social media sites such as Facebook and Twitter are already second nature to them, hence the extensive use of hashtags with this platform. User range in ages from young teenagers all the way through adults in their 30's and even 40's, given that they are technologically savvy at the age.

Given these demographics, Instagram is used by a large number of individuals. Not just in the United States, but on an international scale since it has an Android app too. The total downloads is well over 40 million as of the New Year.

#23 Create an event: putting together an event in which you gather influencers, brand ambassadors, loyal followers, etc. is an excellent way to increase your Instagram followers and definitely a good way of promoting your service. The results of such an event can be multifaceted, such as acquiring an increased number of followers, building increased brand awareness, and increasing engagement with your target audience members.

24 Pose questions: Just like other social media channels, you should ask questions on Instagram. Ask though-provoking questions that make people want to jump in and start interacting. That is exactly how you form relationships. Relationships leads to a good customer satisfaction.

#25 Understand timing in posting on Instagram is very important: As funny as it sounds, there is no universal best time to post on Instagram. This leads us with the question; when should we post on Instagram? Some suggest that around the lunch hour is when people get a break to do what they want and that often includes checking social media. Some would tell you that posting early in the morning is the best. However, you can know your best time by studying your account yourself. When do people hit the like button on your post? When do you receive comments within seconds? Notice the time and stick to it.

#26 Engage with your followers on Instagram live: Instagram live is an awesome avenue to explore if you have the fanbase to do it. Just like Facebook life, you have a great way of interacting with your followers on a personal level. Your live broadcast however should take a few different formats. A few that work well are Q&A's, product launches and influencer takeovers. Whatever the case may be, you should announce your broadcast well in advance on your story, Instagram itself and other social platforms.

Conclusively, you should have a goal for your broadcast. Whether it is to get more followers or more visits to your website or to get more buyers/customers. Have that goal in mind and work towards that specific objective.

27 Prompt followers to turn on post notifications: It may be tough to get your content viewed by your

followers because they are also following several others. You should learn to tell your followers to turn on post notification so that they can get to see your content anytime you post it. This would greatly increase your chances of being seen and would also boost your brand as well as your organic reach. You should think of this the equivalent of an email newsletter for your Instagram feed.

5 Photo Tips To Boost Your

Instagram Marketing

1. Lighting: Bear in mind that no amount of filtering or editing will save a photo that's badly lit. use natural light whenever you can, except in cases where you have access to the right kind of lighting set-up. If you are taking pictures

outside, early morning and late afternoon are the best times.

2. Use your Eyes: Before you take out your phone and start snapping pictures, take a moment to really look at what's going on around you. Use your eyes to structure the photo in your mind. Don't just take out your smart phone and start snapping.

What is in the background of the photo? Is someone about to walk in front of your subject? Is there something going on nearby that might mean taking this picture in a different location would be a better idea? Spend some time looking at your subject, your surroundings, lighting and everything else that is going on before you start clicking away.

3. Use Technology: Instagram provides a variety of filters and editing tools. There are also third party apps which improve the capability of your smart phone camera. There's nothing improper with using apps and tools to take good pictures. Most smart phones have some kind of photo adjusting features and built into their cameras.

They usually include tools that let you cut, switch, modify lighting and contrast levels, increase or decrease saturation, add shadows, shades and highlights and create the long exposure effects.

4. Move around your subject: The lens of smart phone camera soaks up light in a different way in comparison to a traditional camera. When looking through your phone at your subject while moving through a full circle, you'll see how the shifting direction of your light sources can uncover some fantastic effects, and surprising results. You'll start to observe opportunities that previously didn't occur when you just held your phone up and clicked a picture.

5. Change your viewpoint: Shooting from up high or right down on the ground can result in more interesting pictures and makes them look different. Photos that stand out get shared. This is how a single photograph on Instagram can go

viral earn you hundreds or even thousands of followers and help draw attention to your business.

Conclusion

Thank you again for downloading this book! I hope

you learned a lot!

Finally, if you enjoyed this book, then I'd like to ask

you for a favor, would you be kind enough to leave a

review for this book on Amazon? It'd be greatly

appreciated!

Thank you and good luck

Click here (Hyperlink this and put the link of your book on Amazon) to leave a review for this book on Amazon!

Printed in Great Britain
by Amazon